SAMMY RODRIGO

Solo Hiking

Unexpected Lessons From Hiking Alone

Copyright © 2023 by Sammy Rodrigo

All rights reserved. No part of this publication may be reproduced, stored or transmitted in any form or by any means, electronic, mechanical, photocopying, recording, scanning, or otherwise without written permission from the publisher. It is illegal to copy this book, post it to a website, or distribute it by any other means without permission.

Sammy Rodrigo asserts the moral right to be identified as the author of this work.

Sammy Rodrigo has no responsibility for the persistence or accuracy of URLs for external or third-party Internet Websites referred to in this publication and does not guarantee that any content on such Websites is, or will remain, accurate or appropriate.

Designations used by companies to distinguish their products are often claimed as trademarks. All brand names and product names used in this book and on its cover are trade names, service marks, trademarks and registered trademarks of their respective owners. The publishers and the book are not associated with any product or vendor mentioned in this book. None of the companies referenced within the book have endorsed the book.

First edition

This book was professionally typeset on Reedsy. Find out more at reedsy.com

Contents

1	Introduction	1
2	I'll Be Fine	4
3	Unexpected Friendships	12
4	Oh Praise Thee	21
5	That's A Nice Tree	26
6	An Abundance Of Gratefulness	33
7	The Confidence I Didn't Know I Needed	44
8	Getting Into Perspective	50
9	Finding Joy In All Things	59
10	Conclusion	67
About the Author		68

1

Introduction

Have you ever taken a hike alone before? Why or why not? Did someone tell you it wasn't safe? That you could get lost, kidnapped, or hurt? Did a friend cancel on you so you didn't want to go alone?

I have heard dozens of people tell me that they didn't go somewhere or do something because no one else would do it with them. These comments have stuck in my mind and impacted me over the years.

Why? Why do they not go? If you really want to do something, like REALLY want to go to a concert, a restaurant, a new city, or on a new trail why would you just not go?

I believe it's because you're afraid. Maybe you're afraid of not having someone to talk to, how it will look to be standing without someone by your side, or simply not wanting to feel lonely. Maybe it's because you're afraid of your safety. There's bad people out there in the world. There are serious dangers in the world, BUT I truly believe that there is more fear put into people than what is needed.

Overall, I do actually believe it is more fun to do things with others. It's fun to share an experience with someone. You see the tiger roar at the zoo and you turn to your brother and say, "WOW, did you see that? Look!"

You create this beautiful memory you can look back at together and talk about for years to come. When I want to go hiking, to the store, or on a trip I will often ask my family or friends if they want to go with me.

Now you may be thinking, "Wait, I thought the whole point of this book was about doing things alone?" Well yes, you're right. **What I'm trying to say is that doing things with people is preferred BUT if people can't go with you, that doesn't mean you shouldn't go.**

You are missing out on an experience by saying I'm not going to go unless someone else goes with me.

What I have unexpectedly seen over the last 8+ years of my life is that I have learned more about myself while doing things alone instead of when I do them with other people.

When I get time alone to reflect on my life, it brings peace, clarity, and perspective to me. It gives me more space in my mind and life for others. And I just simply enjoy it now.

My hope is that by reading about some of the lessons I have learned it will give you that courage you've been looking for to go on a solo hike or adventure and not say no just because you're alone.

Sammy

INTRODUCTION

Twin Sisters Peak, Estes Park, Colorado

2

I'll Be Fine

It was a cool fall morning in October. I was driving in Rocky Mountain National Park listening to "Take Me Home, Country Roads," singing my duet with John Denver. I always love listening to John Denver when I'm in the mountains, especially when I'm alone. His sweet words and guitar comfort me I guess.

Earlier in the week I wanted to go up into the mountains to see the fall colors. It was already the middle of October and that's when the leaves started to fall already and an early snow storm may turn all the warm yellows and reds a disappointing brown.

I had asked my roommates and a few friends at the time if they wanted to go up to Estes Park that weekend to see the colors. They slowly all gave me reasons they were busy, had previous commitments, or just didn't want to go out of town.

I decided okay, that's fine I still want to go. So that weekend I packed up my things and drove up highway 34 until I saw the Never Summer Mountains greeting me. I wanted to go somewhere new today.

I'LL BE FINE

Somewhere I haven't gone or seen before.

Picking up my park map I traced my fingers along the different roads and trails. My finger was gliding up the road that led to Bear Lake and I stopped thinking about the crowds of people that usually swarm by the lake. I decided to try one of the shorter, less popular trails not so far up the mountains.

When my car pulled up to the trail head there were only 2 other cars there. I grabbed my backpack, water bottle, and jumped out of the car. I started up the trail towards a big grass field without any trees or bushes. I decided not to listen to anything that day. Sometimes I'll listen to music or an audio book, but that day my thoughts filled my head and kept me entertained.

The trail came to a stream that had tall bright yellow aspen trees and red bushes along its banks. It was like a moment from a movie. There was a slight breeze so a few aspen leaves would fall at a time and dance their way down to the water or earth beneath them. I looked up like a little kid with a huge grin on my face smiling. It was so beautiful. So magical.

I continued on the trail for probably an hour and a half before I started to see patches of snow, which surprised me. There wasn't snow in the weather forecast, but it probably snowed last week. As I kept walking there was more snow up on the hills and eventually I got to a point where the snow was completely covering the trail. I couldn't see where I was supposed to go. Since there weren't many people also hiking, there weren't clear footprints for me to follow.

I stopped walking. I looked up the trail and mountains beside me evaluating the situation. This wasn't expected. Snow wasn't in the forecast but I didn't do my research to learn that snow had already fallen. I could continue up the trail but I could get lost and not know my way back.

So I made the decision to turn around. Yes, I probably could have continued and made it to a trail head, a lake or saw other people, but I could have also walked the wrong direction deeper into the woods and gotten lost, not knowing where I was.

Lesson #1 - Be Safe

If you're going to go out into the woods, mountains, or wilderness without another person there are basic safety precautions to take. As much as it used to annoy me when my mom would always say, "Be safe!" whenever I would leave the house, she had a point.

Things don't always go as planned. You get lost. Your phone dies. You twist your ankle. You find someone else that is hurt. You get altitude sickness. You fall into a river and it's cold. It started raining and you didn't bring a rain jacket.

You can't predict every situation that will happen when you go outside, but here are some standard precautions I always take:

- **Check the weather**

I like to check at least 2 sources because sometimes they vary

- **Tell someone where you're going**

Plan to call or text them when you're done. That way if anything happens you're not stuck alone and they can get help

- **Always pack a warm layer**

You can always take a layer off if you're hot, but you can't add what you don't have. I recommend a fleece and waterproof layer jacket.

- **Bring water and a snack**

It's very important to stay hydrated and when your energy gets low have a snack to keep your mood up

- **Wear good, comfortable shoes**

Don't wear new, stiff hiking boots or anything you might get a blister in. I've done this and it sucks. Wear shoes for 30 miles around town before going on a hike in them

- **Pack a map**

It can be on your phone or a paper map, but this is especially important if you've never been there before

- **If it doesn't feel safe get out**

Have common sense and don't push yourself beyond your skill set. If the weather gets really bad and you're not prepared, you need to go back

- **Learn how to act around animals**

When hiking in areas with wild animals, it's important to know how to respond when encountering one. They might be cute but they're also wild

- **Ask for help**

Talk to other hikers and ask how much of the hike is left, what are the conditions towards the top, what trail did they take, did they see any animals, etc

There are great outdoor groups, companies, and online resources where you can learn all kinds of lessons about wilderness first aid, backpacking tips, trail safety, avalanche training, and much more.

I have learned most of my lessons from backpacking in high school and just like anything else in life, you learn with experience! The more you hike and the more you hike with people that do it more than you, the more you will learn. So take a hike!

I'LL BE FINE

I'LL BE FINE

Rocky Mountain National Park, Colorado

3

Unexpected Friendships

It was day two on my road trip. I was heading up through Wyoming to the Pacific Northwest for a friend's wedding. After that, I was going to spend a week camping and hiking in Glacier National Park.

A family friend lived in Jackson, Wyoming and was kind enough to let me stay with her for 2 nights on my journey up north.

I wanted to see the Grand Tetons and knock another national park off my list. I had actually driven past them before and stopped by for an hour but that's never a good way to enjoy a park. It was time to really explore it and see the trails and take in the beauty.

With only one full day in the Tetons my goal was to hike to the base of one of the big mountains with a beautiful lake view. Just like any other hike, I brought my favorite backpack, water bottle, and a few snacks. It was a clear June day with only a few clouds in the sky.

Early into the hike I started going back and forth up the trail with another hiker. I would stop to take my jacket off so he would pass me. Then he would stop to take a sip of water and admire a river, then I would pass him. After about 15 minutes of this, he just turns around suddenly and says, "Hi, I'm John. I'm hiking alone and it looks like you are too. Would you like to hike together?" I appreciated his frankness and said, "Yes!"

We started hiking up together and it was steep early on. Luckily John turned out to be a talker and kept my mind off my burning thighs. John was a nice man, probably in his late forties. He told me he was a doctor back in Rhode Island and was on an "Out West" camping trip with his friend. He talked about his children and that he was dating a woman he met on Christian Mingle that lives in Pennsylvania. How it's hard to find women with good values so he had to look out of state. The distance was hard but he was happy. I liked John. He was honest and open and made me feel comfortable.

While we were hiking up together we saw hills with thousands of wildflowers along the trail. Bright yellows and blues and pinks. We looked behind us and there was a gorgeous clear view of the Jackson Hole valley. Over ¾ of the land is owned and protected by the government so there weren't skyscrapers or suburban neighborhoods, just beautiful land.

After a steep rock scramble we finally made it to the top! We were greeted by a massive granite formation with a soft blue lake under it. Everyone was taking pictures and selfies with the amazing backdrop. John and I took a picture together at the top and he was running short on time and had to leave. We shared how we enjoyed hiking together and he was on his way.

While sitting by the lake at the top, I started talking with two women in their early thirties, Katelyn from Tennessee and Erika from Florida. They were friends from college and came out for a nature trip together. We started comparing the best mountains and hikes in the country. When they asked me if Colorado had mountains like the Tetons I laughed and said, "Yes."

Before I went down, I made sure to not make the same mistake as I did with John and I got their Facebook and Instagram accounts to follow. It can be fun to do that to stay in touch and see what other adventures they go on. Sometimes nothing ever comes from it and you forget who they are over time but on other occasions you chat with each other and become friends. I've even met someone on a trail then visited them when I was on another trip!

While I was hiking down a lady named Katie started talking with me. She was in her late thirties and from Ohio. We talked about our different jobs working in offices, Cuyahoga Valley National Park in Ohio, and my favorite parks in Utah and Colorado.

When I got back to my car, it just so happened that my battery had died and I had to ask two guys in the car next to me to help jump my car.

Lesson #2 - Talk To Strangers

This was one of my most social solo hikes! I got to have genuine conversations with 4 people from 4 different states and I still keep up with several of them on social media.

Not every hike is like that. A year later, I was hiking at the base of Longs Peak in Colorado and the trail was busy. I recall about ⅓ of the hikers were solo hiking like me, but not one person turned around and asked me to be friends with them like John did.

My experience hiking in the Tetons taught me that I actually do like people, at least some people. Talking with a stranger, finding unexpected things in common, learning new things, and sharing that experience together is fun. It feels good to connect with other people. Rather it's just enjoying their company for that short 2 hours hiking together or it turns into a lasting friendship.

If you really want to meet new people intentionally while hiking I would recommend searching for hiking groups on Facebook for specific states or parks you like. I am part of a few and people will ask for hike ideas or hike buddies to go together.

You can hike in very populated trails or parks to be around other people. Or you can just be bold like John and practice asking people to be your friend and talk on the trail! Most people are very friendly and happy because they're outside in a beautiful place. Trying starting a conversation and see where it goes.

SOLO HIKING

Smiling with John at the top of our hike

Delighted by a brilliant field of wildflowers

Overlooking the beautiful expanse of Jackson Hole, Wyoming

Hiking back down with Katie

SOLO HIKING

Grand Tetons National Park, Wyoming

UNEXPECTED FRIENDSHIPS

SOLO HIKING

4

Oh Praise Thee

Have you ever looked close at a honey bee? I don't mean run away from it when you hear it buzzing by your face or start swinging your arms when someone's eyes get big and they yell, "BEE!" I mean really look at them. Study them.

Next time you see a bee on a flower, pause what you're doing and squat down next to it. Look at their delicate little wings. The fuzzy hairs on their legs and abdomen and the bright yellow pollen on their legs that they're loading up to take back to their hive.

When I was in high school, I took a drawing class and remember looking close at a bee one day. I tried to imagine what it would be like to draw that bee. To focus on the shape of their eyes, antennae, head, abdomen, and legs. The intricate detail of their wings and little hairs. I imagined the different color pencils I'd use to pull out the yellows, blacks, browns, and oranges. It made me realize how much attention to detail was put in this one little creature. "Wow," I thought. "This is just ONE bee."

I looked it up and there are 2 trillion bees in the world. 2 TRILLION!

That's 2,000,000,000. I can't even fathom that number. There are also 20,000 species of bees. That's just ONE of the creatures on Earth. There are trillions more bugs and billions of animals, birds, fish, plants, and humans.

Thinking about this made my brain hurt and put me in a state of awe. Taking my focus off of myself and thinking about the natural world was incredibly humbling.

Lesson #3 - Think Less Of Yourself

I believe that it's human nature for people to focus on themselves. In other words, be selfish. We get consumed by it as we think about what we have to do, how we feel physically, what we want to eat, and how others make us feel. Because of this, it's harder to focus on other people and situations unless you really try to.

For me, going outside and hiking is a way to remember life isn't always about me. I can be walking down a trail and hear the birds singing. I look up following their voices and see huge beautiful pine trees with peeling bark and brown pine cones. As I watch a pine cone fall to the ground, I see rocks with twisted colors of red, yellow, and blue from iron, quartz, and algae. As I approach an overlook, I see massive rock formations in front of me, the peaks white with snow. If I look close enough I can see wisps come off the mountain peak from the mighty wind blowing the snow into the air. Pure majesty.

Our world is amazing. It's detailed, designed intentionally, and intricately made.

American theologian John Piper writes, "We are all starved for the glory of God, not self. No one goes to the Grand Canyon to increase self-esteem. Why do we go? Because there is greater healing for the soul in beholding splendor than there is in beholding self."

I don't go outside to hike to the top of a mountain and to think about how awesome I am. I hike to see breathtaking views and feel that sense of awe. I hike to learn more about the natural world and be reminded that I am a small piece of it.

It's so important to do activities that challenge you to look outside of yourself.

May you go for a walk, a hike, a swim and think about how big this world is and how little you are. I hope it will help you see life in a new perspective.

SOLO HIKING

Hiking into the Grand Canyon with my husband Bill

South Kaibab Trail in the Grand Canyon National Park, Arizona

OH PRAISE THEE

The South Rim

Amazed by how GRAND this canyon is

5

That's A Nice Tree

The sun was beating down on me and I was already starting to sweat. For the last two weeks, I had driven from Colorado through southern Utah. I'd seen the towering hoodoos in Bryce Canyon, the massive sandstone walls of Zion, the colorful bark-shaped stone in Petrified Forest, and the delicate remains in several national monuments from desert dwellers hundreds of years ago.

It was November and I was craving warmer weather after sleeping in the car through negative temperatures. However, now that I was in the Tuscan desert I felt weak under the heat like it was sucking up my energy; like it came out of nowhere and startled me. I pulled out my trusty water bottle that is my go-to travel buddy and follows me everywhere. After a few big gulps my energy was already coming back up.

I was staring at my feet walking up the Valley View trail in Saguaro National Park, only an hour and a half from the Mexico-US border. Looking up I was surrounded by a forest of giant cacti. Some of the saguaros were 5 Sammy's tall! There were all kinds of cacti; some looked like long fingers, some looked like a spiky jug of milk, and from a distance some looked like a tall stranger waving at me. There were so many different shapes and shades of green, but all were very pokey with long threatening thorns. "Nature is so cool," I thought.

Continuing up the path I saw a bench indicating an overview was nearing. There were a few dozen tall saguaros at the top of the ridge and as I came to the overview, to my amazement they continued on for miles and miles. There were tens of thousands of saguaros just in my view. I just stood there in awe.

Lesson #4 - Become A Naturalist

After I finally decided it was time to leave the overview, I stopped by the visitor center on the way out of the park and bought a nature guide book. Flipping through its pages, it had descriptions about the stars, birds, rocks, plants, and clouds. I was so excited!

In school, science never was a topic I focused on. Personally, I was always more interested in social studies, English, and art classes. It wasn't until after school when I started to go outside more on my own that I started thinking more about science and the natural world.

Reading my new nature book, I learned basic lessons that were probably taught in my early science classes that I had forgotten after the test. I read about how the world is made up of gasses, liquids, and solids that are all chemicals. How the same chemicals in the air, rocks, and trees are in our human bones and blood. I was amazed. We were all connected. It made sense why going out into nature felt so life-giving.

When I was at that overview in Saguaro National Park, I pulled out my phone and Googled, "how to become a naturalist?" Ads for colleges and programs appeared with bachelor and master degrees. I dreamed about what I wanted to study. "Geology," I thought, "No, geology, astrology, chemistry, biology, and geography. That would be a good start and I can grow from there."

After continuing to research and think about pursuing my new found career in naturalism, it occurred to me that I don't have to drop everything to study nature and change my career. I can continue to learn and ask questions everywhere I go for the rest of my life. It's more about having a curious spirit and a heart that wants to learn and understand. This motivates me to never stop learning and asking questions about our amazing world.

A twisted saguaro cacti, likely 125+ years old

A fishhook barrel cactus eager to bloom

THAT'S A NICE TREE

The average height of an adult saguaro cactus is 40 feet/12 meters

Tall saguaro cacti in the background with Engelman's prickly pear cacti on the left and Staghorn cholla cacti on the right

6

An Abundance Of Gratefulness

The boat was rocking side to side. Even though it was a big boat that could fit 80 people, you could still feel the ocean moving around in your stomach making you feel a little nauseous. Sitting in rows of uncomfortable plastic chairs didn't make it any better. I turned to my friend Isabel, "Let's go out on the deck." We stood up together and walked outside.

Immediately my stomach felt better once the cool ocean breeze hit my face. It was cloudy and misty outside. We were hoping for a clear sunny day, but just happy to be here. We were heading to Santa Cruz & Santa Rosa, both part of the Channel Islands off the coast of California.

"Look!" Isabel screamed. Right next to the boat were a dozen bottle nose dolphins swimming in the wake of the boat. They swam up closer to where we were playing with each other. Suddenly one of them leaped out of the water, twisting in the air before splashing back into the ocean. Another followed then another. People started to cheer and others rushed out of the cabin to see what was going on.

The captain announced we were surrounded by a few pods of dolphins and there were more ahead of us. I looked around the boat and between the crowds on the deck I could see more dolphin bodies leaping out of the water as I imagined them shouting, "Woohoooo, ohh yeaahhh."

I looked at Isabel and we both had huge smiles on our faces. You can't watch dolphins jumping and playing together and not share in feeling their joy of life.

My eyes followed a dolphin swimming away from the boat and my jaw dropped. You could see blue spots jumping out of the water and swimming for miles. There were hundreds of dolphins. The captain announced we had come across a mega pod of over 700 dolphins. I couldn't speak. I was in pure amazement. After taking one video, I put my phone away to just take in the moment. Nothing could capture how incredible it felt or how beautiful it was.

Lesson #5 - Thank You God

That trip to the Channel Islands was incredible. I was so excited to explore the islands when the most amazing part turned out to be the boat ride there. We saw pelicans, 3 species of dolphins, 2 humpback whales, 3 gray whales, giant mola mola fish, and sea lions.

While hiking across Santa Cruz island, I remember turning around and looking across the island. The sky had cleared up just for an hour and the ocean along the coast was shining a brilliant turquoise that bled into the dark indigo of the deeper sea.

A practice that I've made a key part of my daily routine is verbalizing my gratitude. When I wake up in the morning it will usually start with something like,

"Good morning God, thank you for another day of life that was not guaranteed but is a gift. Thank you that I'm safe, warm, dry, healthy, my stomach is full of food, I can get clean water from my sink and I have people in my life that love and care about me."

When I go on a hike, there's almost a trigger that reminds me of how grateful I am for life. I almost can't help it. I take a big deep breath of fresh mountain air (or sometimes ocean air) and feel alive. It's the perfect time to reflect on everything you're grateful for and just be happy.

Looking over Santa Cruz island when the clouds cleared

SOLO HIKING

A group of pelicans by the marina & visitor center

A victory pose at the top of a hike on Santa Rosa Island

Arriving to Santa Rosa Island

A beautiful small tree on Santa Rosa Island

Sea lions enjoying a place to take a nap

Admiring the stone on Santa Rosa Island

A lizard posing by some island flowers

A cave in Santa Cruz Island

Beautiful flowers blooming on a bush on Santa Rosa Island

7

The Confidence I Didn't Know I Needed

It was February in my junior year of college and I didn't have any spring break plans. This is very unlike me because I'm quite the planner. I decided this was unacceptable.

I looked at a U.S. map on my wall with all the national parks and started dreaming of different routes to take. From Northern Colorado, I decided the perfect 1-week trip was to go north to the Dakotas. We'd go see Mount Rushmore, Wind Cave National Park, over to the Badlands in South Dakota and then up to Theodore Roosevelt National Park in North Dakota. On the way back down we could see Devil's Tower National Monument in Wyoming. It was perfect!

So I started texting friends asking who wanted to go with me. Since I was late to planning, most people already had plans or were working. Luckily one friend told me she was interested and later that she wanted to go. I was stoked.

I started researching all the best hikes to go on, where to stay, and must see places. My energy and excitement for the trip kept building, but then a week before spring break my friend canceled on me. I was devastated.

Desperately, I texted a few people to see if I could get any last minute takers but everyone said no. I talked with several people about the trip and it was assumed I wasn't going. You have to have someone to go with you. It's safe. That's normal. It doesn't make sense to go alone.

I can still feel that devastation of canceling a trip that I could have gone on alone because someone else bailed on me. I can feel it. The excitement. The let down. The disappointment. I decided from that moment on I would never not go on a trip that I'm excited to go on, just because no one else can go with me.

That realization really freed me. After that, I started going on more hikes alone. I like hiking and just because I couldn't get someone else to go when my schedule allowed wouldn't stop me from going. At first, I would go on hikes close to town. They were usually only a few miles but it felt refreshing to get out under the sunshine and move. Sometimes it wasn't a "hike," but more like a walk. And that was okay. It was more about enjoying nature and myself.

Then I started going on longer hikes and driving an hour or two away to go for a day or half day hike. The more I went, the more confidence I had to do more alone. It wasn't so scary anymore, I was getting more comfortable. Not just with hiking, but this overflowed to other areas of my life.

I would spend a few hours alone at a coffee shop or park. I would stay in a cabin overnight and read or watch movies. I started flying places to visit friends but I might spend the first few days or several afternoons alone seeing the city, a zoo, a park, or a museum by myself. The more I did things alone, the more normal it felt to me.

Lesson #6 - Have Courage & Go

I have heard dozens of people, usually women, tell me they weren't going to do something because they didn't want to do it alone. They wanted to do something. They wanted to go to that new plant nursery that just opened. They wanted to go to the farmer's market or go see that new movie. They wanted to go skiing or biking. They wanted to. But they chose not to go because they didn't have the self confidence to go alone.

This makes my heart so sad. Not that people want to go places with their friends and share the experience together. I understand that. What makes me sad is people not feeling capable of doing it alone.

For some people, it's a lot harder than others to go out alone or talk to strangers. But no matter who you are, it's hard to be uncomfortable. It makes you feel weird and cringey. Like you have bugs running up and down your back. You just want to shake them off and feel safe and relaxed.

I believe that it's important to push yourself out of your comfort zone. This forces you to grow as a person and makes you stronger. It makes you realize you are capable of more than you previously thought - this is so important!

It opens the doors of your life to see new areas to grow. You can run more than you thought, you can talk to more strangers than you thought, you can get that job you've always wanted, you can have genuine self confidence for the first time, you can not worry about what others think of you.

My recommendation is to start small and build. Remember the lessons from Chapter 1 about being safe. Don't try to run a marathon without training or walk around a big city alone at night.

But maybe that first step is going paddle boarding alone. Or going to a park and laying out a blanket and reading for a few hours without your phone or another person. Or maybe it's booking a trip to Washington DC and staying in a coed hostel - which I did! It was uncomfortable because it stretched me out of my comfort zone sharing a bunk bed room with 12 strangers (8 of which were grown men), but I started talking to them and got to learn about their families and see their personalities and I became more comfortable. Now, I wouldn't be so scared to try something like that because I pushed myself before.

Everyone is different, so my recommendation is to set this book down and write down 3-5 things you can do to challenge yourself. Start small and build.

What will this experience do for you? It will grow and stretch you. It will teach you to have courage. It will make you more independent because you won't be afraid to go out and do things alone anymore. It will show you that you are capable. It will give you a confidence about yourself that you didn't have before! This is what I have experienced that all started from challenging myself to go on a few hikes alone.

Beautiful fall colors in Frisco, Colorado

A forest of dead trees is surprisingly beautiful

Striking a victorious pose while on a solo hike on Mount Royal Trail

Overlooking the valley and beautiful fall colors

8

Getting Into Perspective

My nose and cheeks were burning and tingling from the cold air that felt like ice on my skin. The sun was just starting to come over the mountains but the land was still frozen from the night before.

It was early December and I was hiking up to Emerald Lake in Rocky Mountain National Park. My mom and Aunt invited me to go for a walk that morning, but I actually said, "No, thank you. I really want to go for a hike alone this morning." So I layered up in my warm fleece, green puffy coat, and warm gloves for the crisp winter air.

The beginning of the trail looked like summer. Our warm Colorado sun had melted most of the snow from the trail so if you didn't feel cold air against your face, you may have thought it was May or June. But after a mile up the trail, more snow started to appear until I was walking on it and had to put my micro spikes on the bottom of my shoes.

I love winter hiking. If you wear the right clothes and waterproof shoes, it's comfortable and beautiful. The trail isn't as crowded as it is in the summer and fall. You see a different type of beauty. Instead of green leafy trees, you see tree branches lined with sparkly white snow. It looks as if someone iced the trees with brilliant, shiny icing like on a cake. On the sides of cliffs giant icicles as tall as me dangle next to each other. In the rivers and streams, there are brilliant alpine ice formations of bubbles, cracks, and layers.

It's a great place to admire nature and think. It gives me a place to forget about the basic things that crowd my mind every day and focus on what matters.

Lesson #7: It's Time To Refocus

When I am walking outside my brain feels like it has the space to really think. There are times or temptations when I will think about what I need to buy at the grocery store, who I forgot to email at work, or the next road trip I'm dreaming about going on. It is valuable to think about these things, but on some walks I like to put my "to-do list" items to the side and refocus my life.

I like to think about big picture areas of my life: relationships, dreams, how I feel physically, mentally, emotionally, spiritually. I'll ask myself questions like:

- Who have I not talked to in a long time that I should reach out to?
- Who told me they were going through something that I can follow up with?
- How do I feel physically? Is this where I want to be? What can I do to feel better?
- What family member have I not talked to recently that I can call today?

- Why am I arguing more with my friend? Are there things I need to work on to be a better friend and communicator?
- Am I enjoying my work? What do I imagine or dream about doing in the next few years? What steps do I need to take to get there?

Sometimes I'll pull my phone out as my thoughts are circling in my head and text a friend to ask how they are and follow up on a previous conversation even if it was from months earlier. I may list out things I want to personally work on to improve how I talk to other people, how often I call my parents, what food I eat and how it makes my body feel, or how intentional my prayer life and relationship with God is.

Personally, this time usually is more relationship focused as I try to think outside of my life and imagine what is going on in other people's lives and what it must be like from their perspective. This doesn't come naturally to me so I have to really think about it. I have found it to be an incredible exercise. It allows me to deeply reflect on my relationships, habits and aspirations. It allows me to see areas to grow as a person and care for others around me. And it helps me feel like I can be better centered when I walk back inside my home and start my "to-do list" again.

Nature has become a great place for me to have these self conversations. It has less distractions than in my house and as I've shared, being outside provokes more open minded thoughts for me about the world and others.

Do you ever find yourself asking yourself these questions? Why or why not? Where can you go that doesn't have distractions and can allow you to reflect on your life? I encourage you to try this exercise and see how

GETTING INTO PERSPECTIVE

powerful it can be in helping grow your self awareness, awareness of others, and improve your relationships.

Starting on the trail up to Emerald Lake

GETTING INTO PERSPECTIVE

Emerald Lake - Rocky Mountain National Park, Colorado

SOLO HIKING

Bubbles in the frozen lake

GETTING INTO PERSPECTIVE

Hiking up to Lake Haiyaha

SOLO HIKING

Admiring the majestic snow blowing around the top of the mountains at Lake Haiyaha

9

Finding Joy In All Things

The color of the sun was warm as it was getting closer to the horizon. I was walking down a steep path toward a beach in Montaña de Oro State Park in Central California. I couldn't contain my excitement as I started to hop while trying to remove my shoes. Not willing to stop and properly take them off for fear of missing any time by the ocean.

To my surprise instead of soft, fine sand, the beach was made up of little, colorful pebbles. Shades of blue, yellow, brown, red, black, and white stones ranging from the size of a quarter to a piece of rice.

I walked down the beach toward giant caves that appeared in the cliffs next to the water, peering in to see if there was an end. The sharp rock that lined the dark tunnel made me a little uneasy, wondering what may be inside.

Turning back I headed to the water. Inside of running in, I watched the wake roll up the beach and estimated where the next wave may end. I scooted my toes closer to the end of where the water last touched and waited. The next wave came rushing in bigger than the last and the water shot up my calves and I squealed and laughed.

Putting my shoes back on, I climbed out onto uneven, pokey rock formations that shot out into the ocean. I moved slowly on areas with slippery algae and moved faster excited when I found dry spots. Bending over I studied the mussels cuddling close together surrounded by colorful plants I wasn't familiar with.

While my attention was focused on the mussels, a huge wave came up behind me and sprayed my whole body. I screamed and then giggled jumping from rock to rock. I felt so carefree and happy, like the joy of a small child.

Lesson #8: Have Fun

Going outside, rather I'm alone or with people, is a great way to have fun. You can forget about the busy-ness of your life and enjoy running around in the sun, hiking in the snow, or walking on a path along a beach.

Especially as I have hiked more alone and done more things outside, I have truly come to love the outdoors. It brings me a lot of joy to stop on a trail and admire a beautiful wildflower, studying its curves and colors, and how it's different from the last wildflower I stopped to admire a few minutes earlier.

I love how we can find ways to bring our inner child out jumping around on rocks, swimming in cold mountain lakes, or singing with the birds. It brings out a playful and gentle spirit.

There are so many things you can do outside from hiking, biking, swimming, skiing, rollerblading, climbing, or kayaking. My encouragement is to try several activities and see what you enjoy the most. Find ways to enjoy the outdoors, get some exercise, and have a lot of fun while doing it!

Montaña de Oro State Park

SOLO HIKING

Exploring a small pool that formed on a large rock on the coast

Playing on the sharp rock that reaches out into the ocean

Mussels cuddled together

A rocky beach

SOLO HIKING

Happy Sammy

Montaña de Oro State Park

10

Conclusion

Thank you for reading about lessons I've learned from solo hiking and being outside. I'm grateful for those that have encouraged me, inspired me, and given me advice along the way.

If you enjoyed my stories, I would be very appreciative if you please leave a positive review on Amazon. That means a lot. Thank you.

The outdoors are waiting for you. The trail, river, ocean, and path want you to go experience them. To feel the joy that comes from being outside and feeling refreshed, challenged, and inspired.

Start with setting goals for yourself on things you can do alone and try them! See how it makes you feel. Do them again and notice how it's not as scary. Continue to invite people to do things with you, but don't not do things just because you're alone.

About the Author

Sammy Rodrigo was born and raised in Fort Collins, Colorado and has spent a lot of time in Estes Park and Aspen. Her love for the outdoors grew from backpacking in high school and road tripping with friends in college to their home states back to Colorado.

After visiting state and national parks, it created a fiery joy and passion to visit and explore more and more parks, monuments, and protected nature areas. She loves to share her stories and help others plan road trips to hit all the great must-see spots!

She currently lives in Carbondale, Colorado with her wonderful husband Bill.

You can connect with me on:
- https://www.instagram.com/sammyrodrigo829

Made in the USA
Coppell, TX
23 February 2023